COMFORT *food*

RACHAEL RAY

30-MINUTE MEALS

COMFORT
food

Published by:
Lake Isle Press, Inc.
16 West 32nd Street, Suite 10-B
New York, NY 10001
(212) 273-0796
E-mail: lakeisle@earthlink.net

Distributed to the trade by:
National Book Network (NBN), Inc.
4501 Forbes Boulevard, Suite 200
Lanham, MD 20706
1 (800) 462-6420
www.nbnbooks.com

Library of Congress Control Number: 2005929092

ISBN: 1-891105-23-X

Food photography copyright © 2005 Tina Rupp

Book and cover design: Ellen Swandiak

This book is available at special sales discounts for bulk purchases as premiums or special editions, including personalized covers. For more information, contact the publisher at (212) 273-0796 or by e-mail, lakeisle@earthlink.net

First Edition

Printed in China

10 9 8 7 6 5 4 3

To comfort seekers short on time

Comfort foods, I'm happy to say, are easier to prepare than you think. In less time than it takes to have food delivered, you can have homemade Turkey and Wild Mushroom Meatloaf Patties, classic Chicken Fricassee, or creamy Crab and Corn Chowder. It's all fresh, made with quality ingredients, economical, and always delicious. Cooking brings me joy because it allows me to share something of myself with those I love. It will do the same for you. Enjoy.

Rachael Ray

RACHAEL RAY

30-MINUTE MEALS

DON'T MEASURE WITH INSTRUMENTS, USE YOUR HANDS.

You're not baking or conducting experiments for the government—just feel your way through.

HOW TO MEASURE RACHAEL'S WAY:

A HANDFUL
about 3 tablespoons

❖

A PALMFUL
about 2 tablespoons

❖

HALF A PALMFUL
you do the math

❖

A PINCH
about 1/4 teaspoon

❖

A FEW GOOD PINCHES
about 1 teaspoon

❖

ONCE AROUND THE PAN
about 1 tablespoon of liquid

❖

TWICE AROUND THE PAN
more math: about 2 tablespoons,
3 or 4 would be 1/4 cup

❖

RACHAEL RAY

TOP 30

30-MINUTE MEALS

30-MINUTE
SHEPHERD'S PIE

5-MINUTE
BREAD PUDDING

makes 4 servings

COMFORTfood

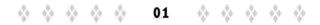
30-Minute **SHEPHERD'S PIE**

2 pounds potatoes, such as russet, peeled and cubed

Salt and freshly ground black pepper

1 tablespoon extra-virgin olive oil

1 & 3/4 pounds ground beef or ground lamb

1 carrot, peeled and chopped

1 onion, chopped

2 tablespoons butter

2 tablespoons all-purpose flour

1 cup beef stock or broth

2 teaspoons Worcestershire sauce

1/2 cup frozen peas

2 tablespoons sour cream or softened cream cheese

1 large egg yolk

1/2 cup cream (vegetable or chicken broth may be substituted)

1 teaspoon sweet paprika

2 tablespoons chopped fresh flat-leaf parsley

In a large pot, boil potatoes in salted water until tender, about 12 minutes.

While potatoes boil, heat a large skillet over medium-high heat. Add oil to hot pan, then beef or lamb. Season with salt and pepper. Brown and crumble meat for 3 or 4 minutes. If you are using lamb and there's a lot of fat, spoon some of it out. Add carrot and onion; cook 5 minutes, stirring frequently. In a second small skillet over medium heat, cook butter and flour together, 2 minutes. Whisk in broth and Worcestershire. Cook to thicken, 1 minute. Add gravy to meat mixture. Stir in peas.

Drain potatoes and pour them into a bowl. Combine sour cream, egg yolk, and cream. Pour the cream mixture into potatoes and mash until potatoes are almost smooth.

Preheat broiler to high. Fill a small rectangular casserole with meat and vegetable mixture. Spoon potatoes evenly over the meat. Top potatoes with paprika and broil 6 to 8 inches from heat until evenly browned, about 2 to 3 minutes. Sprinkle with chopped parsley and serve.

❝After-dinner dancing is highly recommended.**❞**

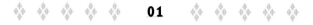

5-Minute **BREAD PUDDING**

1 whole loaf cinnamon-raisin bread
1/4 cup (1/2 stick) butter, softened
1 can (14 ounces) regular or reduced-fat sweetened
   condensed milk
2 jiggers brandy
Whipped cream in canister
Ground or grated nutmeg, for garnish

Heat a griddle pan over medium heat. Cut 4 thick slices cinnamon-raisin bread. Butter both sides with softened butter. Grill until brown and crispy, 2 minutes on each side.

While bread grills, make the sauce: In a small saucepan, heat condensed milk over medium-low heat for 4 minutes. Remove from heat and stir in brandy.

Cut each grilled bread slice into quarters and pile into 4 dessert cups. Top with a few spoonfuls of sauce and a generous swirl of whipped cream. Garnish cream with a sprinkle of nutmeg and serve.

RACHAEL RAY

TOP **30**

30-MINUTE MEALS

TURKEY & WILD MUSHROOM MEATLOAF PATTIES *with* PAN GRAVY

HERB SMASHED POTATOES *with* GOAT CHEESE

SERVE *with* STEAMED GREEN BEANS

makes 4 servings

COMFORT*food*

HERB SMASHED POTATOES
with Goat Cheese

3 large all-purpose potatoes, peeled and cut into chunks
Salt and freshly ground black pepper, to taste
1 tablespoon extra-virgin olive oil
2 tablespoons butter, cut into pieces
1 shallot, chopped
10 blades chives, chopped or snipped (3 tablespoons)
3 or 4 sprigs fresh thyme, leaves stripped and chopped
  (2 tablespoons)
1 cup chicken broth
1 log (4 ounces) herb, peppercorn, or plain goat cheese

Bring a medium pot of water to a boil. Add potatoes and salt. Boil potatoes 15 minutes or until fork-tender. (Begin making meatloaf patties with this pocket of time.)

Drain cooked potatoes and return empty pot to stove. Adjust heat to medium. Add evoo, then butter. When butter has melted, add shallots and sauté, 2 to 3 minutes. Add chives and thyme, then potatoes to the pot. Mash potatoes, adding broth as you work to achieve desired consistency. Season with salt and pepper, to taste.

Cut goat cheese into 4 disks. Serve potatoes on dinner plate and top each mound with a disk of goat cheese.

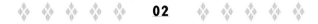
Turkey & Wild Mushroom
MEATLOAF PATTIES
with **Pan Gravy**

3 tablespoons extra-virgin olive oil
8 crimini (baby portobello) mushrooms, chopped
8 shiitake mushrooms, chopped
1 shallot, chopped
Salt and freshly ground black pepper, to taste
1 & 1/3 pounds ground turkey
3 or 4 sprigs fresh sage, chopped (about 2 tablespoons)
1 tablespoon Worcestershire sauce
1/2 cup Italian bread crumbs
1 egg, beaten
2 tablespoons butter
2 tablespoons all-purpose flour
2 cups chicken or turkey broth
1 teaspoon poultry seasoning

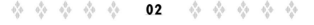

Heat a nonstick skillet over medium-high heat. Add 2 tablespoons evoo, then chopped mushrooms and shallots and season with salt and pepper. Sauté mushrooms, 5 or 6 minutes, until dark and tender. Remove from heat. Transfer mushrooms to a bowl and return pan to heat.

Place turkey in a mixing bowl. Make a well in the center of the meat. Add sage, Worcestershire, bread crumbs, and beaten egg. Scrape sautéed mushrooms and shallots into the bowl. Add salt and pepper. Mix together and make a small, 1-inch patty. Place patty in the hot pan and cook 1 minute on each side. Taste patty and adjust seasonings in meatloaf mixture accordingly.

Divide mixture into 4 equal parts by scoring the meat and form into oval patties, 1-inch thick. Add 1 tablespoon evoo to the pan, add patties, and cook 6 minutes on each side. Transfer to a serving plate.

Return pan to heat and add butter. When butter has melted, whisk in flour and cook a minute or two. Whisk in broth and season with poultry seasoning, and salt and pepper, to taste. Thicken gravy to your liking and pour over patties, reserving a little to pass at the table. Serve alongside herb smashed potatoes and steamed green beans.

RACHAEL RAY

TOP 30

30-MINUTE MEALS

CHICKEN, CHORIZO & TORTILLA "STOUP"

makes 4 servings

COMFORTfood

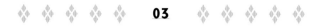

Chicken, Chorizo & Tortilla
"STOUP"

1 pound chicken tenders

Salt and freshly ground black pepper, to taste

3/4 pound chorizo sausage (available in packaged meats section)

2 tablespoons extra-virgin olive oil

2 cloves garlic, smashed

1 medium red bell pepper, chopped

1 medium onion, chopped

8 small red-skinned potatoes, diced

1 can (15 ounces) dark red kidney beans, drained

2 teaspoons hot sauce, such as Tabasco

1 can (15 ounces) chopped fire-roasted tomatoes, such as Muir Glen brand

1 quart chicken broth

1 sack red or blue corn tortilla chips, crushed

2 cups shredded pepper-Jack or smoked cheddar cheese

Chopped scallions, for garnish (optional)

Chopped cilantro, for garnish (optional)

Fresh thyme, for garnish (optional)

Chop tenders into bite-size pieces. Wash up, then season chicken with salt and pepper. Dice chorizo.

Heat a medium soup pot over medium-high heat. Add evoo and chicken to pot. Lightly brown chicken 2 minutes, then add chorizo and garlic. Cook another 2 to 3 minutes, then add peppers, onions, and potatoes. Cook 5 minutes, then stir in beans, hot sauce, and tomatoes. Add chicken broth and bring stoup to a bubble. Reduce heat and simmer until potatoes are tender, 10 to 12 minutes.

Preheat the broiler. Ladle stoup into shallow bowls and top each bowl with a generous handful of crushed tortilla chips and cheese. Melt cheese under hot broiler. Garnish with scallions and herbs, if desired.

RACHAEL RAY

TOP 30

30-MINUTE MEALS

BOURBON-ORANGE CHICKEN *and* SWEET-HOT BUTTER & BREAD

BITTERSWEET DIJON-DRESSED SALAD

makes 4 servings

COMFORTfood

BOURBON-ORANGE CHICKEN
and Sweet-Hot Butter & Bread

Chicken:

2 tablespoons olive or vegetable oil

3 tablespoons butter, cut into small pieces

4 (6-ounce) boneless, skinless chicken breasts

Salt and freshly ground black pepper

1/2 can frozen orange juice concentrate

1/4 cup whole smoked or roasted and salted almonds, chopped

2 shots (3 ounces) bourbon

Butter and Bread:

1 baguette or 4 French dinner rolls

4 tablespoons marmalade

4 tablespoons butter

3 teaspoons hot sauce

Make the chicken: Preheat a medium to large nonstick skillet over medium-high heat. Add oil and butter. The oil will allow the butter to come to a higher temperature without burning the milk solids in the butter. When butter has melted, add chicken. Season with salt and pepper and brown, 3 or 4 minutes on each side. Reduce heat to medium low. Add the juice concentrate and spoon over chicken as it melts down. Simmer 5 minutes. Transfer chicken to dinner plates, leaving most of the sauce in the pan. Top chicken with the almonds.

Raise the heat on the sauce and add bourbon. Cook sauce until it is slightly browned, 2 or 3 minutes. Spoon over chicken and serve.

Make the butter: Place bread in low oven or toaster oven to crisp the crust. In a small bowl, microwave the marmalade and butter 15 seconds on high. Add hot sauce and stir. Spread or brush the sweet-hot butter on the crusty, hot bread and serve alongside the chicken and salad greens.

Bittersweet
DIJON-DRESSED SALAD

2 hearts romaine lettuce, chopped
1 bunch watercress, trimmed, cleaned, and chopped
3 tablespoons orange marmalade
2 teaspoons Dijon mustard
2 tablespoons red wine vinegar
5 to 6 tablespoons extra-virgin olive oil
Salt and freshly ground black pepper, to taste

Mix the romaine and watercress in a medium salad bowl. Whisk together the marmalade, mustard, and vinegar, then whisk in evoo. Pour dressing over the salad and season with salt and pepper. Toss, then adjust seasonings. Mound greens alongside the bourbon chicken and serve.

RACHAEL RAY

TOP **30**

30-MINUTE MEALS

APRICOT CHICKEN

QUICK POTATO & CARROT LATKES

CHUNKY GOLDEN APPLESAUCE

makes 6 servings

COMFORTfood

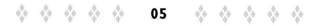

Apricot **CHICKEN**

2 tablespoons extra-virgin olive oil (evoo)
2 pounds chicken tenders, halved on an angle
Salt and freshly ground black pepper, to taste
1 large onion, chopped
2 tablespoons cider vinegar or white wine vinegar
12 dried pitted apricots, chopped
2 cups chicken broth
1 cup apricot all-fruit spread or apricot preserves
2 tablespoons chopped chives, for garnish

Heat a large skillet with a lid over medium-high heat. Add evoo and chicken. Season with salt and pepper. Lightly brown the chicken on each side. Add onions and cook, 5 minutes. Add vinegar to the pan and let it evaporate. Add apricots and broth. When broth comes to a bubble, add preserves and stir to combine. Cover pan, reduce heat and simmer, 10 to 15 minutes. Serve chicken with a sprinkle of chives as garnish.

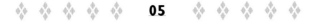
Quick Potato & Carrot **LATKES**

Vegetable oil, for frying

1 sack (24 ounces) shredded potatoes for hash browns (available on dairy aisle)

1 large carrot

1 medium onion

2 eggs, beaten

2 teaspoons salt

1 teaspoon baking powder

3 tablespoons matzo meal, cracker meal, or all-purpose flour

Heat 1/2 inch oil in a large skillet over medium to medium-high heat. To test oil, add a piece of bread to the pan. It should turn golden brown in a count of 10. Adjust heat as necessary.

Place potatoes in a large bowl. Using a hand grater, grate the carrot and onion into the bowl. Add beaten eggs, salt, baking powder, and meal or flour. Combine vegetables and meal with a wooden spoon. Drop mixture into oil in 3-inch mounds. Press down gently with spatula to form patties. Fry in batches of 4 to 6 patties, 1 inch apart, until golden, about 3 minutes on each side. Drain on a paper towel or parchment-lined tray.

"Keep your pots hot!"

Chunky Golden **APPLESAUCE**

4 golden delicious apples, cored and chunked
2 teaspoons lemon juice
1/2 cup golden raisins
1 cup apple juice or cider
3 tablespoons honey

Combine all ingredients in a medium pot and cook over medium to medium-high heat until apples begin to break down and raisins are plump, 10 to 12 minutes. Serve with potato and carrot latkes.

RACHAEL RAY

TOP 30

30-MINUTE MEALS

EVERYTHING JAMBALAYA
on WHITE RICE

makes 4 servings

COMFORTfood

Everything JAMBALAYA
on White Rice

1 cup enriched white rice

1 tablespoon extra-virgin olive oil

1 tablespoon butter

1 pound boneless, skinless chicken thighs or breasts, diced

1/2 pound andouille, chorizo, or linguiça sausage, diced

1 medium onion, chopped

2 ribs celery (from heart of stalk), chopped

1 green bell pepper, seeded and chopped

1 bay leaf, fresh or dried

A few drops hot sauce

2 to 3 tablespoons all-purpose flour

1 can (14 ounces) diced tomatoes

1 can (14 ounces) chicken broth

1 teaspoon ground cumin

1 rounded teaspoon chili powder

1 rounded teaspoon Old Bay seasoning

4 drops each hot sauce and Worcestershire sauce

3/4 pound medium shrimp, peeled and deveined

Coarse salt and freshly ground black pepper, to taste

4 sprigs fresh thyme leaves, stripped from stems and chopped (about 2 tablespoons)

4 scallions, sliced thin

"Food is nostalgia."

Cook rice according to package directions and keep covered.

Place a large, deep skillet over medium-high heat. Add oil to pan and melt butter into it. Add chicken and brown 2 minutes. Add sausage and cook 2 minutes more. Add onion, celery, bell pepper, bay leaf, and a few drops of hot sauce. Sauté veggies 'til tender, another 3 to 5 minutes. Sprinkle flour over vegetables and chicken and cook a minute more, while stirring. Add tomatoes and broth to pan and combine well. Season with cumin, chili powder, Old Bay seasoning, and 4 drops each of hot sauce and Worcestershire.

Scatter shrimp into pot and cook until pink and firm and sauce thickens a bit, about 3 minutes. Season with salt and pepper to taste.

To serve, ladle jambalaya into bowls. Using an ice cream scoop, place 1 scoop of rice in the center of each bowl of jambalaya. Top with chopped thyme and scallions.

RACHAEL RAY

TOP 30

30-MINUTE MEALS

VEAL INVOLTINI
WITH PANCETTA
on BED OF SPINACH

makes 4 servings

COMFORTfood

VEAL INVOLTINI with Pancetta
on Bed of Spinach

1 pound veal scaloppini

1/4 cup chopped fresh flat-leaf parsley

Salt and freshly ground black pepper, to taste

1 pound smoked fresh mozzarella cheese, thinly sliced

1 jar (16 to 18 ounces) roasted red peppers, drained and sliced

1/3 pound sliced pancetta or thin-cut bacon

2 tablespoons extra-virgin olive oil, plus more for drizzling

1 clove garlic, cracked

1 sack (10 ounces) baby spinach or triple-washed spinach leaves

1/4 to 1/3 cup white wine or dry vermouth

Arrange scaloppini on waxed paper or plastic wrap. Sprinkle with parsley, salt, and pepper. Place a thin layer of cheese and a few slices of roasted pepper on each scaloppini. Roll veal and wrap each roll with a slice of pancetta. Secure with toothpicks.

Fry veal rolls in a thin layer of evoo until golden all over and pancetta is crisp, 5 or 6 minutes. Remove from pan to a warm platter. Return skillet to heat. Add a drizzle evoo and the garlic to pan. Wilt spinach in pan, add a touch of wine or vermouth to lift drippings and combine them with greens.

Using tongs, place a bed of spinach on each dinner plate and top with veal rolls. Serve immediately.

RACHAEL RAY

TOP 30

30-MINUTE MEALS

ALL-AMERICAN PATTY MELTS

SERVE *with* GREEN SALAD *or* SLAW

makes 4 servings

COMFORTfood

All-American PATTY MELTS

1 pound ground sirloin
2 rounded tablespoons dill pickle relish
2 tablespoons steak sauce
1 tablespoon Montreal Steak Seasoning by McCormick
2 teaspoons sweet paprika
A drizzle of extra-virgin olive oil
3 tablespoons butter, divided
1 large onion, thinly sliced
8 slices rye, white, or pumpernickel bread
8 deli slices Swiss cheese

Heat a large nonstick skillet over medium-high heat.

Mix meat and relish, steak sauce, steak seasoning, and paprika. Divide meat and form 4 large, thin patties.

Add evoo to pan and cook burgers 3 or 4 minutes on each side. Take patties out and add another drizzle of evoo and 1 tablespoon butter. When butter has melted into oil, fry onions until just tender, 5 minutes. Slide onions onto patties.

Return pan to the stove and add the 1 tablespoon butter and 2 slices of bread. Top each bread slice with a slice of cheese, a patty with onions, and another slice of cheese. Top each sandwich with another slice of bread

"Always season to taste."

and press the patty melts together. Cook 2 or 3 minutes on each side to set the sandwich and toast the bread.

Add remaining tablespoon butter to pan and repeat process to make 2 more sandwiches. Cut sandwiches from corner to corner. Serve with chips of choice and greens or slaw dressed with oil, vinegar, salt, and pepper.

RACHAEL RAY

TOP 30

30-MINUTE MEALS

TURKEY CORN CHILI

SERVE *with* TORTILLA CHIPS

makes 4 servings

COMFORTfood

TURKEY CORN CHILI

l medium onion, chopped

1 tablespoon corn or vegetable oil

2 cloves garlic, chopped

1 & 1/3 pounds ground lean turkey

1 small red bell pepper, seeded and chopped

1 & 1/2 cups frozen corn kernels

1 can (32 ounces) diced tomatoes

3 scallions, chopped

1 teaspoon poultry seasoning

1 & 1/2 tablespoons chili powder

1 tablespoon ground cumin

1 to 2 ounces hot sauce to taste

Coarse salt and freshly ground black pepper, to taste

Shredded cheese, such as cheddar, for topping

In a deep saucepot over medium-high heat, sauté onion in oil for 3 to 5 minutes.

Add garlic and cook 1 minute more. Add turkey and brown 5 minutes. Add bell pepper, corn, and tomatoes. Bring to a bubble, stirring in scallions, spices, hot sauce, and salt and pepper.

Reduce heat and simmer 10 minutes.

Serve in bowls topped with cheese and tortilla chips on the side.

RACHAEL RAY

TOP 30

30-MINUTE MEALS

RETRO-METRO FANCY TUNA CASSEROLE

ICEBERG LETTUCE SALAD *with* TANGY TOMATO-TARRAGON "FRENCH" DRESSING

makes 4 servings

COMFORT *food*

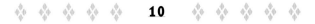

ICEBERG LETTUCE SALAD *with*
Tangy Tomato-Tarragon "French" Dressing

Salad:

1 large head iceberg lettuce, chopped

1/4 seedless cucumber, sliced

1 cup shredded carrots (preshredded are available in sacks in produce section)

A few cherry or grape tomatoes

Dressing:

3 tablespoons white wine vinegar

2 teaspoons sugar

1 rounded tablespoon tomato paste

2 tablespoons chopped fresh tarragon or 2 teaspoons dried tarragon

1/3 cup extra-virgin olive oil

Salt and freshly ground black pepper, to taste

Combine lettuce, cucumber, carrots, and tomatoes in a salad bowl. In a small bowl, combine vinegar and sugar, then whisk in tomato paste. Add tarragon and whisk in evoo in a slow, thin stream, then season dressing with salt and pepper. Pour dressing over salad, toss, and serve.

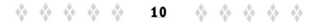

Retro-Metro FANCY TUNA CASSEROLE

1/3 loaf day-old crusty bread or 1 day-old crusty roll

1 pound extra-wide egg noodles or 1 box (12 ounces) egg fettuccini

2 (1 pound) tuna steaks

1 cup white wine

1 bay leaf

A few whole peppercorns

1 tablespoon extra-virgin olive oil

4 tablespoons butter

1 large shallot, chopped

12 white mushrooms, thinly sliced

Salt and freshly ground black pepper, to taste

1 teaspoon ground thyme or poultry seasoning

2 tablespoons all-purpose flour

1 & 1/2 cups chicken broth

1 cup heavy cream or half-and-half

1 cup baby frozen peas

Chopped fresh flat-leaf parsley, for garnish

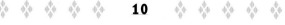
Place bread in toaster oven on medium heat to dry and toast, 20 minutes. Bring a large pot of water to a boil. Add salt, then pasta. Cook according to package directions to al dente. Drain.

Place tuna in a small skillet and add wine; add just enough water to cover fish. Add bay leaf and peppercorns. Bring liquids to a boil. Reduce heat to simmer and cover skillet. Poach fish 12 minutes.

Meanwhile, heat a large, deep skillet over medium heat. Add evoo and 2 tablespoons of the butter. Add shallots and mushrooms and season with salt and pepper. Sauté gently 5 minutes. Sprinkle in thyme and flour and cook 1 minute, stirring with a whisk. Whisk in chicken broth, then cream. Adjust seasonings. Add peas.

Remove poached tuna to a bowl and flake with a fork.

Add noodles and tuna to sauce. Remove from heat and transfer mixture to a casserole or serving dish.

Use the biggest holes on a box grater to grate the bread into large crumbs. Melt remaining 2 tablespoons butter in a small cup in microwave and pour melted butter over bread. Scatter bread crumbs and parsley over the top of the casserole. Serve immediately.

RACHAEL RAY

TOP **30**

30-MINUTE MEALS

TURKEY CUTLETS *with* CRANBERRY-ORANGE STUFFING *and* QUICK PAN GRAVY

BOURBON-PECAN SMASHED SWEET POTATOES

SERVE *with* STEAMED BROCCOLI

makes 4 servings

COMFORTfood

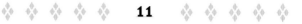

TURKEY CUTLETS *with* Cranberry-Orange Stuffing *and* Quick Pan Gravy

Stuffing:

1 tablespoon extra-virgin olive oil (evoo)

2 tablespoons butter, cut into small pieces

2 ribs celery with leaves (from heart of stalk), chopped

1 medium onion, chopped

1 bay leaf, fresh or dried

Salt and freshly ground black pepper, to taste

2 cranberry-orange muffins (from bakery)

A few sprigs fresh thyme, leaves stripped and chopped (2 tablespoons)

1 cup chicken broth

Turkey and Gravy:

1 & 1/3 pounds turkey breast cutlets

Salt and freshly ground black pepper, to taste

1 teaspoon poultry seasoning

2 tablespoons extra-virgin olive oil (evoo)

2 tablespoons butter, cut into small pieces

2 tablespoons all-purpose flour

2 cups chicken broth

Chopped fresh flat-leaf parsley, for garnish (optional)

Make the stuffing: To a medium frying pan over medium heat, add evoo and butter. When butter has melted, add celery, onion, and bay leaf. Season with salt and pepper. Split muffins and crumble into pan to combine with vegetables. Add thyme and chicken broth. Cook 5 minutes, then remove from heat and let stand in warm pan.

Prepare the turkey and gravy: Preheat a large nonstick skillet over medium-high heat. Season cutlets with salt, pepper, and poultry seasoning. Add evoo and sauté cutlets 5 minutes on each side. Transfer to a warm plate and cover with aluminum foil.

Return skillet to stove and reduce heat a bit. Add butter, then flour to the melted butter. Cook flour and butter a minute or two, stirring with a whisk. Whisk in chicken broth. Reduce the broth, 2 or 3 minutes, to desired gravy consistency. Season with salt and pepper, to taste.

To serve, mound stuffing onto dinner plates using an ice cream scoop. Rest sautéed turkey cutlets on top of stuffing and cover turkey with gravy. Garnish with chopped parsley and serve with smashed sweet potatoes and steamed broccoli.

"WOW, is this stuff good!"

Bourbon-Pecan
SMASHED SWEET POTATOES

3 medium sweet potatoes, peeled and cut into chunks

3 tablespoons butter, cut into small pieces

1/2 cup chopped pecans

3 tablespoons brown sugar

2 shots bourbon

1/2 cup orange juice

1/4 to 1/2 teaspoon freshly grated nutmeg

Salt and freshly ground black pepper, to taste

Bring a medium pot of water to a boil. Add sweet potatoes and cook, 12 to 15 minutes, until very tender. Drain sweet potatoes in a colander. Return pot to medium heat and add butter. When butter has melted, add pecans and toast, 2 minutes. Add sugar; let it bubble. Add bourbon and cook out alcohol, 1 minute. Add orange juice and sweet potatoes to the pot.

Smash with a masher and season with nutmeg, salt, and pepper.

RACHAEL RAY

TOP 30

30-MINUTE MEALS

GRANDPA'S ZITI
with SAUSAGE &
CANNELLINI BEANS

SERVE *with* CRUSTY BREAD *and*
GREEN SALAD

makes 4 servings

COMFORTfood

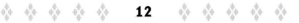

GRANDPA'S ZITI *with* Sausage &
Cannellini Beans

1 & 1/2 pounds bulk Italian sausage, 3/4 pound sweet and 3/4 pound hot

2 tablespoons extra-virgin olive oil

4 to 6 cloves garlic, minced

1 small white onion, finely chopped

1 can (28 ounces) crushed tomatoes

1 can (14 ounces) Italian-style diced tomatoes

20 fresh basil leaves, roughly cut or torn

1 can (15 ounces) cannellini beans, drained and rinsed

1/2 pound ziti rigate (with lines), cooked until al dente

Grated Parmigiano or Romano, for the table

In a deep skillet or frying pan, brown crumbled sausage over medium-high heat. Remove from pan to a paper towel-lined dish to drain. Return the pan to heat, reducing heat to medium-low. Add olive oil, garlic, and onion; cook 5 minutes, until onion softens. Add tomatoes, basil, and beans. Heat through. Return sausage to sauce. Drain pasta and combine with sauce. Serve with plenty of grated cheese, crusty bread, and a green salad.

RACHAEL RAY

TOP 30

30-MINUTE MEALS

CRAB & CORN CHOWDER CUP-O-SOUP *with* CHEESY MUFFINS

makes 4 servings

COMFORTfood

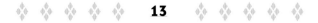

CRAB & CORN CHOWDER CUP-O-SOUP *with* Cheesy Muffins

<u>Chowder:</u>

2 tablespoons butter

2 slices thick-cut bacon, chopped

1 medium onion, chopped

1/2 red bell pepper, chopped

2 ribs celery with leaves, chopped

4 sprigs fresh thyme

Salt and freshly ground black pepper, to taste

2 teaspoons hot sauce, such as Tabasco

2 tablespoons all-purpose flour

2 teaspoons Old Bay seasoning

3 cups half-and-half

2 cups chicken broth

1 cup frozen shredded potatoes for hash-browns (available on dairy aisle)

6 ounces lump crabmeat, broken up

1 cup frozen corn kernels

Chopped chives or fresh flat-leaf parsley, for garnish

<u>Muffins:</u>

2 sandwich-size English muffins, split

8 ounces extra-sharp white cheddar cheese, sliced

In a medium pot over medium-high heat, melt butter. Add bacon, onion, bell pepper, celery, and thyme. Season with salt, pepper, and hot sauce and cook 5 minutes. Stir in flour and Old Bay and cook a minute more.

Whisk in half-and-half, then add broth. Bring soup to a bubble, then stir in potatoes. Simmer until potatoes are cooked and soup has thickened enough to coat the back of a spoon, about 15 minutes. Add crabmeat and corn.

Heat toaster oven or broiler and toast English muffins. Top each muffin with cheese and return to oven to melt cheese.

Remove thyme stems from the soup (the leaves will have fallen off). Stir and adjust seasonings. Pour soup into mugs. Garnish with chives or parsley. Serve soup with cheesy muffin for dipping.

RACHAEL RAY

TOP 30

30-MINUTE MEALS

CHICKEN FRIED STEAKS
with **CREAMED PAN GRAVY**
& BISCUITS

SERVE *with*
STEAMED GREEN BEANS

makes 4 servings

COMFORT food

CHICKEN FRIED STEAKS
with Creamed Pan Gravy & Biscuits

1 package bake off biscuits (such as Pillsbury)
  prepared to package directions
2 round steaks, 1/2-inch thick (1 & 1/2 pounds total)
Wax paper
1 cup plus 2 tablespoons flour
1/3 cup cornmeal
1 teaspoon sweet paprika
1 teaspoon salt
1/2 teaspoon freshly ground black pepper
2 eggs, beaten
2 tablespoons water
4 tablespoons vegetable oil
2 tablespoons flour
1 & 1/4 cups beef broth or stock
1/4 cup half-and-half or cream

Preheat a large, heavy skillet over medium-high heat.

Set steaks on a wax-paper-lined work surface and cover
with another piece of wax paper. Pound steaks to a 1/4-
inch thickness. Set steaks aside. Line work surface with
more wax paper. Pour 1/2 cup flour into each of two
piles on opposite ends of this work space. Add cornmeal, paprika, salt, and pepper to one pile of flour. Beat

"With cooking, the most important tip is to relax."

eggs and water in a pie plate or shallow dish.

Cut steaks in half and coat first in plain flour, then in egg, and then in the seasoned flour and cornmeal mixture.

Add 2 tablespoons oil to hot skillet and brown 2 steaks at a time. As they brown, remove from the pan, and add more oil, as needed. When the last 2 portions are browned, add the first two back to the pan. Cover pan, lower heat to medium-low and cook covered, 15 minutes.

Remove steaks to serving platter and pour off all but 2 to 3 tablespoons of drippings. Add 2 tablespoons flour to the drippings, and cook, 2 minutes. Whisk in broth and season with salt and pepper. Add half-and-half or cream and whisk into gravy. When gravy bubbles, remove from heat. Top steaks and warm biscuits with gravy and serve with steamed green beans.

RACHAEL RAY

TOP 30

30-MINUTE MEALS

THE ONLY RECIPE
YOU NEED: CARBONARA

SERVE *with* GREEN SALAD

makes 4 servings

COMFORTfood

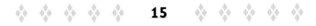

 15

The Only Recipe You Need:
CARBONARA

Salt and freshly ground black pepper, to taste
1 pound rigatoni
1/4 cup extra-virgin olive oil (evoo)
1/4 pound pancetta, chopped
1 teaspoon crushed red pepper flakes
5 or 6 cloves garlic, chopped
1/2 cup dry white wine
2 large egg yolks
1/2 cup grated Romano cheese, such as Locatelli
A handful of finely chopped fresh flat-leaf parsley, for
    garnish (optional)

Put a large pot of water on to boil. Add a liberal amount of salt and rigatoni; cook to al dente, about 8 minutes.

Meanwhile, heat a large skillet over medium heat. Add evoo and pancetta. Brown pancetta 2 minutes. Add red pepper flakes and garlic and cook 2 to 3 minutes more. Add wine and stir up all the pan drippings.

Beat yolks, then add 1 large ladleful (about 1/2 cup) of the pasta cooking water. This tempers the eggs and keeps them from scrambling when added to the pasta.

Drain pasta well and add it directly to the skillet with pancetta and oil. Pour the egg mixture over the pasta. Toss rapidly to coat the pasta without cooking the egg.

Remove pan from heat and add a big handful of cheese, lots of pepper, and a little salt. Continue to toss and turn the pasta until it soaks up egg mixture and thickens, 1 to 2 minutes. Garnish with parsley, if desired, and extra cheese. Serve with green salad on the side.

RACHAEL RAY

TOP 30

30-MINUTE MEALS

PUMPKIN &
BLACK BEAN SOUP

CHUNKY GUACAMOLE

SERVE *with* TORTILLA CHIPS

makes 4 servings

COMFORTfood

PUMPKIN & BLACK BEAN SOUP

1 tablespoon vegetable or canola oil
1 tablespoon butter
1 medium onion, finely chopped
1 can (14.5 ounces) chicken or vegetable broth
1 can (14.5 ounces) diced tomatoes in juice
1 can (15 ounces) black beans, drained and rinsed
1 can (15 ounces) pumpkin puree
1/2 cup heavy cream
1 & 1/2 teaspoons curry powder
1 teaspoon ground cumin
3 pinches cayenne pepper (1/4 teaspoon)
Coarse salt, to taste

Heat a deep pot over medium heat. Add oil and butter.
When butter melts, add onion and sauté, 5 minutes, until
tender. Add broth, tomatoes, black beans, and pumpkin.
Bring to a boil, reduce heat to low and stir in cream,
curry powder, cumin, cayenne, and a few pinches salt.
Simmer 5 minutes and adjust seasonings. Serve with
chunky guacamole and tortilla chips.

"The way to anyone's heart is still through his (her) stomach.**"**

CHUNKY GUACAMOLE

2 medium ripe avocados, pitted and diced
The juice of 1 lemon
1 jalapeño pepper, seeded and finely chopped
1/2 small onion, finely chopped
Coarse salt, to taste

Mash avocado with lemon juice into a chunky paste. Stir in jalapeño, onion, and salt, to taste. Serve with tortilla chips for dipping.

RACHAEL RAY

TOP 30

30-MINUTE MEALS

QUICK TAGINE-STYLE CHICKEN *with* COUSCOUS

SERVE *with* GREEN SALAD *and* FLAT BREAD

makes 4 servings

COMFORT*food*

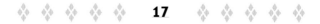

QUICK TAGINE-STYLE CHICKEN *with* Couscous

<u>Chicken:</u>

2 tablespoons extra-virgin olive oil (evoo)

4 cloves garlic, smashed, skins discarded

1 & 3/4 pounds boneless, skinless chicken breasts, cut into large bite-size pieces

1 tablespoon Montreal Steak Seasoning, or coarse salt and freshly ground black pepper

2 medium yellow onions, quartered and sliced

10 pitted prunes, coarsely chopped

1/4 cup golden raisins (1-ounce box)

2 cups low-sodium chicken broth

<u>Spice blend:</u>

1 & 1/2 teaspoons cumin

1 & 1/2 teaspoons sweet paprika

1/2 teaspoon coriander

1/2 teaspoon turmeric

1/8 teaspoon cinnamon

<u>Couscous:</u>

1 can (14 ounces) chicken broth (about 2 cups)

2 cups couscous

2 tablespoons extra-virgin olive oil

2 scallions, finely chopped

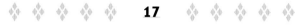
Garnishes:

Chopped cilantro leaves or fresh flat-leaf parsley

Finely chopped scallions

Mango chutney

Make the chicken: Heat a large nonstick skillet over medium-high heat. Add evoo and smashed garlic. Scatter chicken around the pan in an even layer. Season with steak seasoning, or salt and pepper. Cook chicken pieces 2 minutes on each side to brown, then add onions, prunes, raisins, and broth. Mix spices in a small dish and scatter over the pot. Cover and reduce heat to moderate. Cook 7 or 8 minutes; remove the lid and stir.

Prepare the couscous: Bring chicken broth to a boil in a medium pot. Add couscous, evoo, and scallions, and remove from the stove immediately. Cover and let stand 5 minutes. Fluff with a fork.

Uncover chicken and cook another 2 to 3 minutes to thicken sauce slightly. Adjust the seasoning to taste and place chicken on a bed of couscous with chopped cilantro and chopped scallions for garnish. Serve with mango chutney. A green salad and flat bread will complete the meal.

RACHAEL RAY

TOP 30

30-MINUTE MEALS

ITALIAN-STYLE
MAC 'N CHEESE

SERVE *with* GREEN SALAD

makes 4 servings

COMFORTfood

Italian-Style MAC 'N CHEESE

Salt and freshly ground black pepper, to taste

1 pound ziti rigate, penne rigate, or cavatappi

1 pound Italian bulk sweet sausage

2 tablespoons extra-virgin olive oil

1 tablespoon butter

3 or 4 cloves garlic, chopped

12 crimini mushrooms, sliced

2 tablespoons flour

1 cup chicken stock

1 cup heavy cream

2 & 1/2 cups (10-ounce sack), shredded Italian
  4-cheese blend

1 can diced tomatoes, well drained

1 teaspoon hot sauce, such as Tabasco (optional)

1/2 cup grated Parmesan cheese

"Pasta is my favorite way to fill a belly.**"**

Bring a large pot of water to a boil. Salt water and cook pasta just to al dente, about 8 minutes.

In a nonstick skillet, brown and crumble the sausage. Drain cooked crumbles on a paper towel-lined plate. Return pan to heat and add evoo, butter, garlic, and mushrooms. Season liberally with salt and pepper. Sauté 3 to 5 minutes, until mushrooms are lightly golden.

Preheat broiler to high.

To mushrooms, add flour and stir, cooking 2 minutes. Whisk in stock, then stir in cream. Bring cream to a bubble, then stir in 2 cups of 4-cheese blend. When cheese has melted into sauce, add tomatoes. When sauce comes to a bubble, remove from heat and adjust seasonings, adding hot sauce, if desired.

Combine cheese sauce with sausage and pasta, transfer to a baking dish, casserole, or ovenproof serving platter. Sprinkle remaining 1/2 cup of 4-cheese blend and the grated Parmesan over the top and brown under hot broiler. Serve with green salad on the side.

RACHAEL RAY

TOP 30

30-MINUTE MEALS

PORK CHOPS *with* GOLDEN APPLESAUCE

CREAMY CORN

LEMON-SCENTED BROCCOLINI

makes 6 servings

COMFORTfood

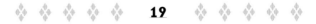

PORK CHOPS
with Golden Applesauce

Applesauce:

4 golden delicious apples, chopped

1 teaspoon grated lemon zest

2 teaspoons fresh lemon juice

2 ounces golden raisins (a handful)

1 inch fresh gingerroot, peeled and grated

3 tablespoons light brown sugar

2 cups natural apple juice or cider

1/2 teaspoon cinnamon

1/4 teaspoon grated fresh nutmeg

Pork chops:

2 tablespoons vegetable oil or olive oil

6 center-cut boneless pork loin chops, 1-inch thick
(6–8 ounces each)

Salt and freshly ground black pepper

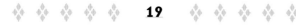
Make the applesauce: Combine apples, lemon zest, lemon juice, raisins, ginger, brown sugar, apple juice, cinnamon, and nutmeg in a medium pot over medium-high heat. Cook until a chunky sauce forms, 10 to 12 minutes, stirring occasionally. If sauce begins to spatter, reduce heat a little, but allow sauce to reduce and form quickly. Once apples are soft and sauce forms, remove from heat.

Heat a large nonstick skillet over medium-high heat. Add oil to the pan. Season chops on one side with salt and pepper. Using a pair of tongs, add chops to hot oil, seasoned side down. Season top side with salt and pepper, too. Brown and caramelize 2 minutes on each side, then reduce heat to medium and cook until juices run clear, another 5 to 6 minutes, turning occasionally. Remove from heat and let chops rest a couple of minutes, allowing juices to redistribute. Top with generous portions of warm golden applesauce to serve.

Lemon-Scented **BROCCOLINI**

1 & 1/2 pounds broccolini
1 cup water
4 strips lemon peel
Salt, to taste

Place broccolini in a skillet. Add water and tuck lemon peels in and around the broccolini. Cover and bring to a boil, then add a little salt. Keep covered and cook until tender, 6 to 7 minutes. Drain and serve.

CREAMY CORN

5 or 6 ears fresh corn or 2 boxes (10 ounces each)
   frozen corn kernels, thawed

2 tablespoons butter

1 rib celery with leaves, chopped

1/2 small red bell pepper, chopped

2 scallions, chopped

2 tablespoons fresh thyme leaves

Salt and freshly ground black pepper, to taste

1/2 cup half-and-half

Scrape corn kernels from cobs, if using.

Heat a medium skillet over medium heat. Add butter and let it melt; add celery, bell pepper, and scallions and lightly sauté for 3 minutes, then add corn and season with thyme, salt, and pepper. Cook 5 minutes, then add half-and-half. Cover and cook over medium-low heat for 10 minutes. Uncover and stir, then adjust seasonings.

RACHAEL RAY

TOP 30

30-MINUTE MEALS

PASTA *al* FORNO

SERVE *with* GREEN SALAD

makes 4 servings

COMFORTfood

PASTA *al* FORNO

Salt and freshly ground black pepper, to taste
1 pound ziti rigate or penne rigate (with lines)
Softened butter, for greasing baking dish
2 tablespoons extra-virgin olive oil
1 small onion, finely chopped
3 cloves garlic, chopped
1 can (15 ounces) crushed tomatoes
1/2 cup heavy cream
2 pinches cinnamon
3 ounces prosciutto (one thick slice), chopped
1/4 to 1/3 cup grated Parmigiano Reggiano cheese

Bring large pot of water to boil, add salt and cook pasta
to al dente, 7 minutes. Once pasta water comes to a
boil, preheat oven to 500°F.

Butter a medium-size baking dish or casserole. To a
medium skillet over medium heat, add evoo. Cook onions
and garlic in evoo, 3 to 5 minutes. Stir in tomatoes and
bring to a bubble. Add cream and season with cinnamon, salt, and pepper. Add prosciutto and pasta to
sauce, stirring to combine. Adjust seasonings and transfer to buttered baking dish. Cover with cheese and bake
10 minutes. Serve hot, with green salad on the side.

RACHAEL RAY

TOP 30

30-MINUTE MEALS

MINESTRA
(BEANS & GREENS)

SERVE *with* CRUSTY BREAD

makes 4 servings

COMFORTfood

MINESTRA (Beans & Greens)

<u>Meat-Free Minestra:</u>

1/4 cup extra-virgin olive oil

8 cloves garlic, chopped

1 medium onion, chopped

2 medium heads escarole greens (about 1 & 1/2 pounds), washed, dried, and coarsely chopped

3 cans (14 & 1/2 ounces each) cannellini beans, drained

1 quart (32 ounces) vegetable broth

1/2 teaspoon ground nutmeg

Coarse salt and freshly ground black pepper, to taste

Lots of grated Parmigiano, Romano, or Asiago cheese, for the table

<u>Minestra with Meat:</u>

Substitute chicken broth for vegetable broth and add the following ingredients:

1/4 pound pancetta (Italian bacon, available at deli counter), or 1/4 pound center-cut bacon, chopped

1/4 pound prosciutto, chopped

1/4 pound capocollo ham, chopped

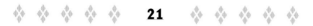

Heat a deep skillet over medium heat. Add oil and garlic. When garlic speaks by sizzling in oil, add onion and meats, if you are using them. Sauté for 5 minutes.

Add escarole and turn with tongs until completely wilted. Add beans and broth. Stir in nutmeg, salt, and pepper. Partially cover pot and let cook 10 minutes.

Serve with lots of grated cheese and warm, crusty bread.

RACHAEL RAY

TOP 30

30-MINUTE MEALS

SWEDISH MEATBALLS & EGG NOODLES

SERVE *with* GREEN SALAD

makes 4 to 6 servings

COMFORTfood

SWEDISH MEATBALLS & EGG NOODLES

<u>Meatballs:</u>

1 & 1/3 pounds ground chuck, or ground beef, pork, and veal mix

3/4 cup bread crumbs

1 egg, beaten

1 small onion, finely chopped

A few drops Worcestershire sauce

Salt and freshly ground black pepper, to taste

<u>Sauce:</u>

3 tablespoons butter

2 tablespoons all-purpose flour

1/2 cup dry sherry

1 & 1/2 cups beef stock

Freshly ground black pepper, to taste

1 teaspoon Dijon mustard

1 cup sour cream, or reduced-fat sour cream

1 rounded tablespoon red currant or grape jelly

1 pound wide egg noodles, cooked to package directions

2 tablespoons butter, cut into small pieces

A handful chopped fresh parsley

Place a pot of lightly salted water on the stove to boil and cook egg noodles once the water has come to a rapid boil. Meanwhile, make meatballs and sauce.

To bake meatballs: Preheat oven to 400ºF. Mix ingredients for meatballs in a large bowl. Form bite-size balls and place on nonstick cookie sheet. Bake 12 minutes.

To cook meatballs on the stovetop: Preheat a large nonstick frying pan over medium heat. Mix ingredients for meatballs in a medium-size bowl. Form bite-size balls and add directly to the pan as you roll them. Once the last ball has been added, give the pan a good shake and cover with a lid or aluminum foil. Cook 10 to 12 minutes, turning meatballs occasionally by giving the pan a good shake. Remove to a paper towel-lined plate, wipe out pan, and return pan to heat to make the sauce.

To make sauce: Melt butter over medium heat. Sprinkle in flour and whisk continuously until a smooth paste is formed and mixture begins to darken a bit. Slowly add sherry while continuing to whisk; cook until sherry reduces by half. Add broth in a slow stream and continue to stir until sauce thickens enough to lightly coat the back of a spoon and is glossy in appearance. Turn off heat and whisk in pepper, Dijon mustard, sour cream, and jelly, mixing well.

Toss hot egg noodles with butter and parsley. Coat meat-balls in sauce and serve over noodles, with green salad on the side.

RACHAEL RAY

TOP 30

30-MINUTE MEALS

ROSEMARY GRILLED CHICKEN *and* WILD MUSHROOM SAUCE

RIBOLLITA—BREAD SOUP

makes 4 servings

COMFORTfood

Ribollita–Bread SOUP

2 tablespoons extra-virgin olive oil, plus some for
   drizzling at the table

4 large cloves garlic, chopped

1 medium onion, chopped

2 carrots, peeled and diced

2 ribs celery, chopped

1 fresh or dried bay leaf

Coarse salt and freshly ground black pepper, to taste

2 cans (15 ounces each) small white beans, such as
   Goya brand

6 cups chicken stock or broth

2 cups tomato sauce

3 cups stale chewy Italian bread, crust removed and
   bread torn into pieces

1 small white onion, finely chopped, for garnish

1 cup grated Parmigiano Reggiano cheese

Heat a deep, heavy-bottomed pot over moderate heat. Add oil, garlic, onion, carrots, celery, and bay leaf to the pot. Season with salt and pepper and sauté until veggies begin to soften, 5 to 7 minutes. Add beans, stock, and tomato sauce. Cover pot and bring soup to a boil over medium-high heat. Remove lid and stir in torn stale bread. Continue stirring. When soup becomes thick and bread is distributed evenly, adjust seasonings. Remove bay leaf. Some ribollitas are so thick, the spoon can stand upright. Make yours as thick or as thin as you like by using more bread or more stock or water. Remove bay leaf.

Serve soup in shallow bowls and top with raw onion, a drizzle of olive oil, and a generous sprinkling of grated Parmigiano Reggiano.

Note: Cannellini beans may be substituted, but look for cans marked "small white beans" on international foods aisle of market.

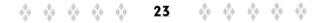

ROSEMARY GRILLED
CHICKEN *and* Wild Mushroom Sauce

Chicken:

1 & 1/2 pounds boneless, skinless chicken thighs

Extra-virgin olive oil, for drizzling

Coarse salt and freshly ground black pepper, to taste

3 stems fresh rosemary, leaves stripped and chopped

Sauce:

1 cup chicken or vegetable stock

1 ounce dried porcini mushrooms

2 tablespoons extra-virgin olive oil

1/8 pound (4 slices) pancetta, chopped (available at deli counter) or 3 slices bacon, chopped

2 cloves garlic, crushed

1 large shallot, chopped

2 portobello mushroom caps, halved and thinly sliced

Coarse salt and freshly ground black pepper, to taste

1 tablespoon flour

1 cup dry red wine

Heat a grill pan over high heat. Drizzle chicken thighs with oil, season with salt, pepper, and rosemary. Grill chicken 5 minutes on each side or until no longer pink and remove from heat to rest.

Place stock in a small bowl and cover. Heat in microwave on high for 2 minutes. Remove from microwave with oven mitt. Add dried porcinis to stock, replace the cover, and steep 5 to 10 minutes. Or, if using stovetop, simmer broth and dried mushrooms for 10 minutes over low heat.

In a medium skillet, add olive oil and sauté pancetta, garlic, and shallot over medium heat for 3 minutes to crisp pancetta at edges. Add sliced portobellos, season with salt and pepper, and sauté 10 minutes, or until dark and tender. Add flour and cook 1 minute. Add red wine to the pan and reduce by half, 1 minute. Add reserved stock and porcini mushrooms and simmer together a minute or two longer.

Slice chicken thighs and fan out on a plate. Ladle thick mushroom sauce down over sliced chicken and serve.

RACHAEL RAY

TOP 30

30-MINUTE MEALS

CHILI MAC

SERVE *with* GREEN SALAD

makes 4 servings

COMFORTfood

CHILI MAC

2 pounds ground sirloin
2 tablespoons extra-virgin olive oil (evoo)
1 sweet onion, chopped
2 jalapeño peppers, seeded and chopped
4 cloves garlic, chopped
3 tablespoons dark chili powder
2 tablespoons cumin
2 tablespoons hot sauce, such as Frank's Red Hot
Coarse salt, to taste
1 cup beer or beef broth
1 can (28 ounces) diced tomatoes in juice
1 can (14 ounces) crushed tomatoes
1 pound corkscrew-shaped or elbow pasta with lines,
  cooked to al dente and drained
Chopped scallions, for garnish

In a big, deep pot, brown beef in evoo over medium-high heat. Add onions, peppers, and garlic. Season with chili powder, cumin, hot sauce, and salt. Cook 5 minutes, then stir in beer or broth, reduce liquid by half, 2 minutes. Stir in both cans of tomatoes and simmer.

Add hot pasta to pot and stir to coat pasta evenly. Remove from heat and garnish big bowlfuls of chili mac with chopped scallions. Serve with green salad on the side.

RACHAEL RAY

TOP 30

30-MINUTE MEALS

SUPER-STUFFED
MONTE CRISTO SANDWICHES

SERVE *with* SLICED FRUIT

makes 4 servings

COMFORTfood

Super-Stuffed
MONTE CRISTO SANDWICHES

8 slices center-cut or applewood-smoked bacon
4 large eggs, beaten
1/4 cup half-and-half, warmed
1/4 teaspoon grated fresh nutmeg or ground
1/2 teaspoon freshly ground black pepper
2 tablespoons butter
8 thick slices soft whole-grain, white, or challah bread
1/2 cup brown mustard
1/2 cup whole-berry cranberry sauce
1/2 pound deli-sliced Havarti cheese
1 pound deli-sliced ham
1 pound deli-sliced turkey breast
1 & 1/2 cups medium to dark amber maple syrup

Heat a griddle pan or large skillet over medium-high heat.
Cook bacon until done, 5 minutes, and remove to paper
towels. Drain off fat. Reheat griddle over medium heat.

Beat eggs with half-and-half, nutmeg, and pepper. Add 1
tablespoon butter to the griddle and let it melt. Turn 4
slices bread in egg batter then place on griddle. Turn
bread after it browns, 2 to 3 minutes; spread mustard on
2 slices bread and top the other 2 slices with cranberry

sauce. Place a slice of cheese on each slice of bread. Add 2 slices bacon, ham, and turkey to bottoms then set tops in place and press sandwiches together. Turn a couple of times and let set a minute or two to melt cheese. Repeat to make 2 more sandwiches. Cut sandwiches from corner to corner to serve.

Heat syrup in microwave-safe container for 30 seconds. Cut sandwiches from corner to corner. Drizzle syrup over sandwiches at the table, or serve in small ramekins for dipping. Serve with a side of sliced fruit.

RACHAEL RAY

TOP 30

30-MINUTE MEALS

MY MAMMA'S ASPARAGUS RISOTTO

SERVE *with* GREEN SALAD

makes 4 servings

COMFORTfood

My Mamma's ASPARAGUS RISOTTO

6 cups vegetable or chicken broth
1 cup asparagus tips
2 cloves garlic, minced
3 tablespoons extra-virgin olive oil
3 tablespoons butter
1 small cooking onion, chopped
2 cups Arborio rice
1/2 cup dry white wine
1/2 cup grated Parmigiano Reggiano or Romano cheese
Coarse salt and black pepper, to taste

Place broth in a medium saucepan. Bring to a slow boil, reduce heat to lowest setting, and let simmer.

Meanwhile, steam asparagus in 1/2 cup of water for 2 minutes, then drain. In a medium skillet over medium heat, sauté asparagus until tender with garlic and 2 tablespoons olive oil. Set aside.

In a deep saucepan or skillet, melt butter into remaining tablespoon olive oil over medium heat. Add onion and sauté, 3 to 5 minutes until tender. Add rice and sauté, 2 minutes more. Add the wine (a couple of glugs) and let evaporate, 2 minutes. Add 1 cup of broth and let it get

"God tells mammas just about everything, the rest they figure out."

absorbed by the rice. Keep adding small amounts of remaining broth to the pan, stirring frequently until absorbed. Taste rice after 15 to 17 minutes and only add as much broth as needed to cook the rice al dente—tender, but with a little bite left to it. Remove from heat and stir in cheese and asparagus. Season with salt and pepper, to taste. Serve with green salad on the side.

RACHAEL RAY

30-MINUTE MEALS

VEAL CHOPS *with* PEPPERS

SERVE *with* GREEN SALAD

makes 4 servings

COMFORTfood

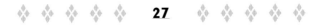

VEAL CHOPS *with* Peppers

4 bone-in veal chops (1/2-inch thick)

Salt and freshly ground black pepper

3 tablespoons extra-virgin olive oil (evoo)

4 cloves garlic, smashed away from skins

3 cubanelles (Italian sweet peppers), sliced

1/2 cup dry white wine

2 hot cherry peppers, chopped

2 to 3 tablespoons juice from cherry pepper jar

Chopped fresh flat-leaf parsley, for garnish

Preheat oven to 375°F.

Heat a skillet with an ovenproof handle over medium-high heat. (If you don't have an ovenproof skillet, double-wrap the handle tightly in aluminum foil.) Season chops with salt and pepper. To hot skillet, add 2 tablespoons evoo, then the chops. Brown 2 minutes on each side; remove to a plate.

Add the remaining tablespoon evoo to the pan, then the garlic and sweet peppers. Cook until soft, 3 to 5 minutes, then add the wine. Return chops to the pan with the peppers and transfer to the oven. Cook 12 to 15 minutes or until juices run clear near the bone. Remove pan from oven and add cherry peppers and a splash of pepper juice. Transfer chops to a serving platter. Spoon juices and peppers evenly over the chops and garnish with parsley. Serve with green salad on the side.

RACHAEL RAY

TOP 30

30-MINUTE MEALS

QUICK CREOLE SHRIMP *with* WHITE RICE

SERVE *with* GREEN SALAD *and* GARLIC TOAST

makes 4 generous servings

COMFORTfood

Quick CREOLE SHRIMP
with White Rice

2 cups water

1 cup enriched white rice

2 tablespoons vegetable oil

4 small ribs celery with leaves (from heart of stalk),
    chopped

1 medium onion, chopped

1 medium green bell pepper, seeded and chopped

4 large cloves garlic, chopped

2 tablespoons flour

2 bay leaves, fresh or dried

2 sprigs fresh thyme, chopped (about 1 tablespoon) or
    1 teaspoon dried thyme

1 can (28 ounces) diced tomatoes in juice

3 to 4 dashes Worcestershire sauce (about 1 teaspoon)

6 to 8 dashes hot sauce, such as Tabasco (about 2
    teaspoons)

Coarse salt and freshly ground black pepper, to taste

2 pounds large fresh shrimp, peeled and deveined

4 scallions, chopped, to garnish

"Cooking is a natural form of self expression.**"**

Bring 2 cups water to a boil in a medium pot; add rice, and bring back to a boil. Cover, reduce heat to low, and simmer 20 minutes.

While rice cooks, place a deep skillet or heavy-bottomed pot over medium to medium-high heat. Heat oil and add celery, onion, green pepper, and garlic. Cook veggies 5 minutes to soften and sweeten. Sprinkle pan with flour, add bay and thyme leaves, and cook another 2 or 3 minutes. Stir in tomatoes, Worcestershire, Tabasco, and salt and pepper. Bring to a bubble, then toss in shrimp. Partially cover pot and allow to stew for 10 minutes, or until rice is done.

Fluff rice with a fork, and remove from heat. To serve, ladle shrimp and sauce into shallow bowls. Using an ice cream scoop, place a mound of rice in the center of each bowl of shrimp. Sprinkle with chopped scallions. The rice is placed on top of the shrimp to prevent it from becoming mushy. Serve with green salad and garlic toast.

Note: Peeled and deveined raw shrimp is available at many supermarkets; just ask your seafood manager for it. It's often not in the case, but they can get it for you.

While I love this recipe for my Nanny's Creole shrimp, you should know that there are as many ways to make this dish as there are Southern cooks. Be creative—add chili powder, lemon juice, whatever floats your shrimp boat!

RACHAEL RAY

TOP 30

30-MINUTE MEALS

BUCATINI
ALL'AMATRICIANA

SERVE *with* GREEN SALAD

makes 6 servings

COMFORTfood

BUCATINI all'Amatriciana

2 tablespoons extra-virgin olive oil

1/4 pound (4 or 5 slices) pancetta, chopped

1 medium onion, chopped

4 to 6 cloves garlic, chopped

1 teaspoon crushed red pepper flakes

1 can (28 ounces) crushed tomatoes

2 tablespoons chopped fresh flat-leaf parsley

Salt and freshly ground black pepper, to taste

1 pound bucatini (hollow spaghetti)

Grated Parmigiano Reggiano, grana padano, or
   Romano cheese, to pass at table

Bring a large pot of water to a boil.

Meanwhile, heat a large, deep skillet over medium-high heat. Add evoo and pancetta. Cook pancetta 2 or 3 minutes, then add onions, garlic, and red pepper flakes. Cook until onions are translucent, 7 or 8 minutes. Add tomatoes and parsley. Season with salt and pepper. Simmer over low heat until ready to serve.

Add salt and pasta to boiling water. Cook pasta to al dente, about 10 minutes. Drain pasta well (do not rinse; starchy pasta holds more sauce) and toss with sauce. Pass grated cheese at the table and serve with green salad on the side.

Note: Pancetta is Italian rolled, cured pork, similar to bacon, but not smoked. Look for it at your deli counter. Bacon may be substituted; it will result in a smoky-tasting tomato sauce.

RACHAEL RAY
TOP 30
30-MINUTE MEALS

CHICKEN FRICASSEE

SERVE *over*
SPLIT BISCUITS
or RICE PILAF

makes 4 servings

COMFORTfood

CHICKEN FRICASSEE

4 prepared buttermilk biscuits or 1 package
  (6.9 ounces) rice pilaf, such as Near East brand,
  cooked to package directions

1 to 1 & 1/3 pounds boneless, skinless chicken breast
  (4 breast halves)

1/2 teaspoon poultry seasoning

Coarse salt and freshly ground black pepper, to taste

1 tablespoon extra-virgin olive oil, plus a drizzle more

1 tablespoon butter

2 medium carrots, peeled, and chopped fine

4 scallions, chopped

1 large shallot, chopped fine

1/2 cup dry white wine (or add an extra 1/2 cup
  chicken broth instead)

1 cup chicken broth

3 or 4 sprigs fresh tarragon, very thinly sliced (about 2
  tablespoons)

2 to 3 tablespoons superfine flour, such as Wondra brand

"A little music adds to any party and relaxes every cook. Mix it up!**"**

Season chicken with poultry seasoning and salt and pepper. Lightly brown chicken in the tablespoon of olive oil, 4 or 5 minutes per side, over medium to medium-high heat in a large nonstick skillet. Remove chicken, cut into large bite-size pieces, and set aside.

Add a little more oil and butter to pan. Add veggies and sauté 5 minutes. Add wine or 1/2 broth and allow it to reduce by half, 1 or 2 minutes.

Pour in 1 cup broth and stir in tarragon. In a small bowl, combine superfine flour with a splash of broth or water and stir into a thin paste. Add paste to pan and combine with juices using a whisk. Slide chicken back into pan and cook until meat is tender yet cooked through and sauce is thickened to desired consistency, 3 or 4 minutes. Adjust seasonings to taste with salt and pepper.

Serve over split biscuits or prepared rice pilaf.

Index